SPIDERS
AND THEIR
WEB SITES

by **Margery Facklam**

Illustrated by **Alan Male**

Little, Brown and Company
Boston   New York   London

Other books in this series:

The Big Bug Book
Creepy, Crawly Caterpillars
Crabs and Other Crusty Creatures

To my grandchildren, in order of appearance: Jeffery, Christopher,
Michael, Katherine Ann, Daniel, Alex, Matthew, and Brian
And to Dr. Wayne Gall, entomologist at the Buffalo Museum of Science,
and Mrs. Loewer's class at Clarence Center Elementary School,
who helped us learn about spiders
— M. F.

To my daughters, Sophie and Chloe
— A. M.

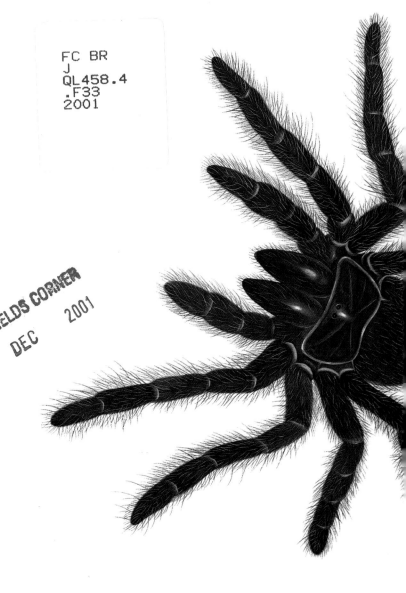

Text copyright © 2001 by Margery Facklam   Illustrations copyright © 2001 by Alan Male

First Edition

Library of Congress Cataloging-in-Publication Data
Facklam, Margery.
    Spiders and their web sites / by Margery Facklam ; illustrated by Alan Male. — 1st ed.
    p.   cm.
    Summary: Illustrations and text provide a close-up look at the physical characteristics and
habits of twelve different spiders and of daddy longlegs.
    ISBN 0-316-27329-5
    1. Spiders — Juvenile literature. [1. Spiders.] I. Male, Alan, ill. II. Title.
QL458.4.F33   1999
595.4'4 — dc21   97-43822

10 9 8 7 6 5 4 3 2 1

TWP

Printed in Singapore

CONTENTS

A DOZEN SPIDERS (PLUS ONE THAT'S NOT)

People who create computer Web sites to attract attention or catch new customers are borrowing an idea millions of years old. Even before there were dinosaurs, spiders were luring insects to their web sites.

How could such delicate little animals have survived for so long in a world full of bigger creatures? The answers are silk and venom. All spiders spin several different kinds of silk, which they use for nets, draglines, traps, doormats, nests, egg sacs, sleeping bags, balloons, wrapping tape, and weapons. And all spiders make venom to paralyze or kill their prey.

No matter where you are, there is a spider not far away. More than 35,000 different kinds of spiders have been identified. They live in every part of the world; some of them in your attic, backyard, and basement. Some people are afraid of spiders, but spiders are more friend than foe. Without them, we could be overrun with insects. At certain times of year, two million spiders may be living in one acre of wild meadow, and each spider eats at least one insect a day. In the United States and Canada, only two kinds of spiders are dangerous. But when you know where they live, it's easy to stay away from them.

All you need for spider watching is a flashlight and a magnifying glass. Once you get a close look at the dozen spiders on these pages, plus one that's not a spider, you won't want to run away from them.

SCORPION

WHITE CRAB SPIDER

NURSERY WEB SPIDER

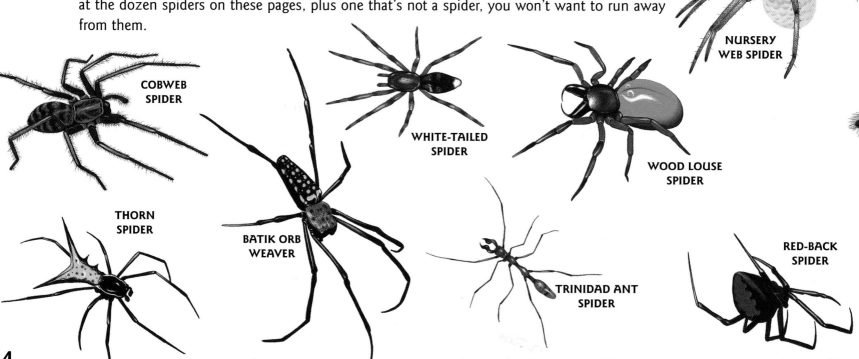

COBWEB SPIDER

WHITE-TAILED SPIDER

WOOD LOUSE SPIDER

THORN SPIDER

BATIK ORB WEAVER

TRINIDAD ANT SPIDER

RED-BACK SPIDER

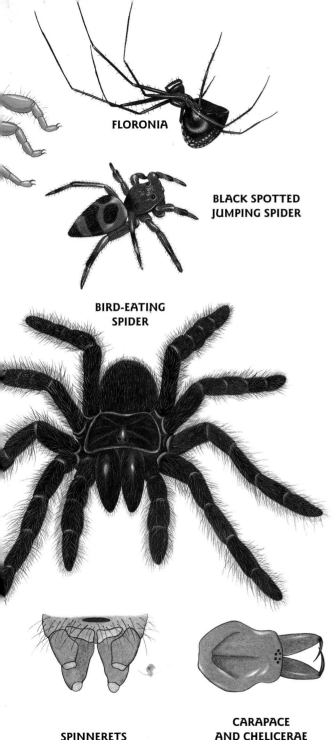

FLORONIA

BLACK SPOTTED
JUMPING SPIDER

BIRD-EATING
SPIDER

SPIDER PARTS

Spiders are not insects. They belong to a huge group of animals called *Arthropoda* (ar-THRAW-puh-duh), along with insects, crabs, and other animals that have jointed legs and get their shape from an *exoskeleton* instead of an inner skeleton of bones. An exoskeleton can't stretch, so arthropods have to molt or shed this covering when it gets too tight for their growing body.

All spiders have eight legs. Most of them have eight eyes, but some have six. Spiders have no antennae. Their bodies are divided into two parts: the abdomen and the *cephalothorax* (se-fuh-luh-THOR-ax), which is the head and thorax combined. The spider's pincer-like jaws, called *chelicerae* (ki-LI-suh-ree), are found on the cephalothorax and have two fangs that inject venom. The four pairs of legs are also attached to the cephalothorax. Between the chelicerae and the first pair of legs, spiders have a pair of *pedipalps*. These "palps" look like short legs, but they are used more like arms, to hold on to things.

On their rear ends, spiders have two or three pairs of *spinnerets,* which spin out silk made by glands in their abdomen. Each gland makes a different kind of silk, which oozes out as a liquid from hundreds of tiny nozzles on the spinnerets. The silk hardens as the spider pulls on it. Scientists once thought liquid silk became solid when it hit the air, but now they know that *tension* causes it to harden. The harder the spider tugs on it, the stronger the silk will be. A spider can move its spinnerets wide apart to make wide bands of *swathing* silk for wrapping prey or bring them close together to make a thin thread. They can make silk that is fluffy, or tough and dry, or that sticks like Velcro.

PLACEMENT OF EYES

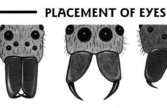

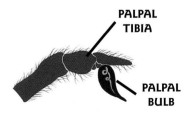

PALPAL
TIBIA

PALPAL
BULB

SPINNERETS

CARAPACE
AND CHELICERAE

FANG AND
POISON DUCT

HUNTING
SPIDER

JUMPING
SPIDER

CRAB
SPIDER

PALP

GARDEN SPIDER

Most spiders are clothed in dull, drab colors, the better to hide themselves. But the orange-and-black garden spider, *Argiope* (ar-JEE-uh-pee), hangs head down like a bright bull's-eye in the middle of its big orb web. As an extra attraction, *Argiope* adds a wide zigzag ribbon of silk through the center of its web. Why does it make this fancy ribbon? It may be a warning to keep birds from crashing into the web, or perhaps it makes the web stronger. Or it may be a way to lure insects into the spider's parlor. In the ultraviolet rays of sunlight, an insect's compound eyes see things differently from the way we do. The zigzag pattern in the web may look enough like a flower to attract an insect hungry for nectar.

There are almost as many kinds of webs as there are spiders, but the orb web spiders such as *Argiope* are especially good engineers. A spider starts an orb web by floating out a silk line and waiting for it to touch down on some object. Then with dry, unstretchy silk, it spins a sturdy frame and a temporary spiral. When the spider goes back to put in the sticky trap lines, it moves from spoke to spoke, biting off the dry lines, recycling the old silk by eating it, and tapping down the new sticky silk to fasten it securely. A spider works an hour or more to make a web and may use as much as 200 feet of silk.

Spiders don't get stuck in their own webs, because they have an oily covering on their legs, and their feet end in little claws and bristles that can grip thin silk threads. But web builders also leave a space between the hub and sticky threads as a free zone, where they can cross the web without getting stuck when they dash out to bite a trapped bug.

Spiders don't make up their own web designs. Those are built-in and automatic for each *species*. But spiders do adjust and shape their webs to fit different sites and situations. In 1973, Arabella and Anita were the first orb web spiders in space. Aboard *Skylab II*, in zero gravity, their first webs were tangled and crooked. But after they got used to space travel, their orb webs were as fine as any on Earth.

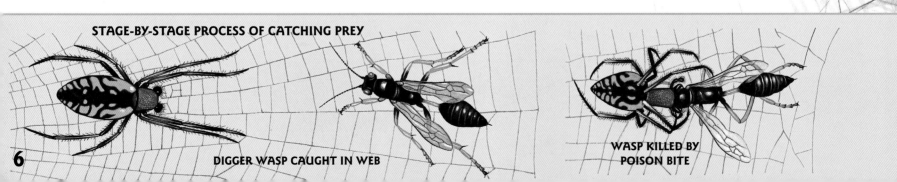

STAGE-BY-STAGE PROCESS OF CATCHING PREY

DIGGER WASP CAUGHT IN WEB

WASP KILLED BY POISON BITE

PREY WRAPPED IN SILK AND LEFT TO BE CONSUMED LATER

GOLDEN SILK SPIDER

The web of the golden silk spider, *Nephila*, is so strong that it can trap a bird in flight or entangle a person running through the woods. In woodland clearings of the Gulf Coast of Alabama and northern Florida, *Nephila* spiders the size of saucers often spin orb webs as wide as garage doors.

The people of the South Sea Islands, in the Pacific Ocean, know how to trick *Nephila* into making fishing nets for them. They bend long bamboo poles in a loop at one end and stick the other end in the ground. During the night the spiders weave their thick webs on these handy frames. In the morning, the islanders pull the bamboo sticks out of the ground and go fishing with their spider-made nets.

Spider silk is stronger than any other natural fiber. It is stronger than steel wire of the same thickness and stretchier than nylon or rubber. A strand of silk would have to be 50 feet long before it would break under its own weight. Because *Nephila*'s silk is twice as strong as the silk made by silk moth caterpillars, many people have tried to use the spiders to make cloth. But it takes more than an hour for one person to reel in 150 yards of silk from one spider held in a little harness. At that rate it would take 5,000 spiders to spin enough thread to make one dress. And just think of how many flies would be needed to feed all those spiders.

But spider silk has other uses. Before we had stick-on bandages, people put spiderwebs on cuts to stop the bleeding. Now we know why that didn't cause infections: a substance in spider silk keeps fungus and bacteria from attacking cobwebs, even old ones.

In World War II, engineers used spider silk to make fine crosshairs for accurate bombsights in bomber planes. Now, in a lab at the University of Rochester in New York state, scientists shoot powerful laser beams at a chemical pellet to create the kind of nuclear power made by the sun. Spider silk holds this tiny target in place better than steel or any other material. When the scientists need silk to tie a new pellet in place, a spider is nudged from its perch to spin a dragline they can collect. In other labs, scientists are trying to copy the proteins in spider silk in order to make strong, stretchy, lightweight fibers that could be used for such things as better bullet-proof vests for police officers and soldiers.

SPINNERETS

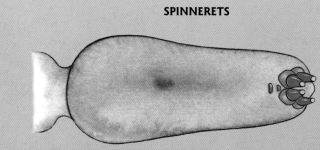

STAGES OF WEB CONSTRUCTION

FISHING SPIDERS

Many lightweight spiders can run short distances across water without sinking, because they hold their body high and tiptoe on long, skinny legs. But one kind of spider is built for fishing. In England, it is called a raft spider, because people once thought that it made a little raft from leaves. While that's not true, its heavy body resting on the water does look something like a raft.

A fishing spider always anchors a dragline to the shore before it rows across the water, using its second and third pairs of legs as oars. When it wants to make a quick stop, it just grabs the line with one of the little claws on a hind leg and pulls up right next to its prey.

You can find these big spiders hanging around docks and bridges. They usually dangle the first and second pairs of their long legs in the water the way barefoot kids cool their feet. Like a bobber that bounces in the water to signal a hooked fish tugging on the end of a line, the spider's feet pick up vibrations that signal an insect landing on the water, and the spider darts across the surface to catch it. When stronger vibrations signal a pollywog or minnow swimming near the surface, the fishing spider doesn't hesitate to dive underwater to catch it.

One kind of fishing spider can actually live underwater, because it carries its own air tank. Like all spiders, the European water spider gets oxygen through a special set of lungs, called *book lungs,* on the underside of its abdomen. Book lungs are arranged in layers like pages in a book, with air-filled spaces between the layers of blood-filled tissues that take the oxygen from the air. When the European water spider swims underwater, its book lungs are always covered by a bubble of air that clings to its hairy abdomen. With this portable air supply, the spider has no trouble searching for a meal below the water.

The water spider also makes an air-filled underwater house, where it rests and eats its prey. First it weaves a bell-shaped web and anchors it to a plant. Then it pops up through the surface of the water, grabs an air bubble between its rear legs, and dives under again. It lets go of the bubble where it will float up to fill the web. A water spider's summer house is a temporary shelter close to the surface of the water. But in winter, it makes a sturdier house on the bottom of the pond or stream, where it won't be damaged by ice or wind.

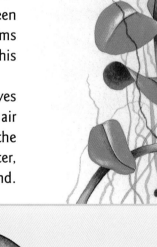

FISHING SPIDER
ONE OF THE LARGEST AQUATIC SPIDERS; LIVES ON SURFACE AND
DARTS UNDERWATER TO CATCH PREY, USUALLY FISH/TADPOLES

BOOK LUNGS

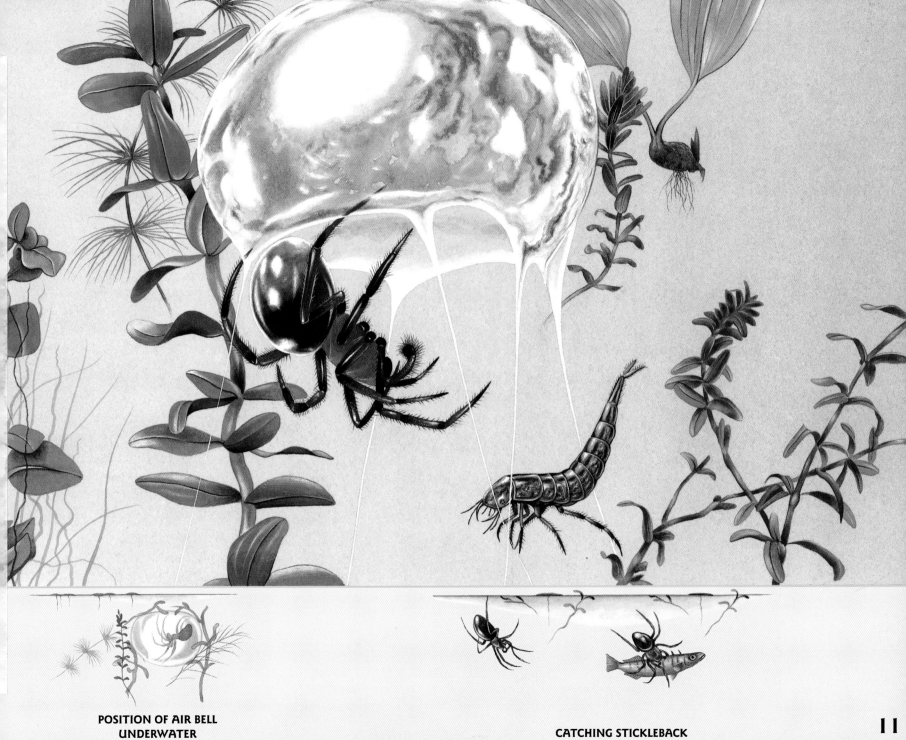

**POSITION OF AIR BELL
UNDERWATER**

CATCHING STICKLEBACK

11

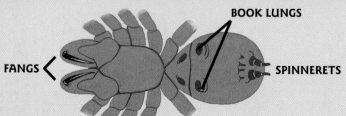

FANGS 〈

BOOK LUNGS

SPINNERETS

UNDERSIDE

POISON DUCT

FANG

CHELICERAE

ACT IN UNISON AND FACE DOWNWARD

12

TARANTULA

Tarantula! Some people get the shivers just saying the word.

But one kind of tarantula, with pink toes and a velvety brown coat, seems too dressed up to be scary. Some people even keep these fuzzy, pink-toed spiders as pets. The Mexican red-leg tarantula is another favorite pet because it has a gentle nature, and with good care, it can live for twenty years. The names of some of the 800 different tarantulas describe them perfectly, such as red-rump, orange-knee, and starburst baboon. The Goliath tarantula is so big that if it sat in the center of a dinner plate, its feet would hang over the edge. You'll only meet this super-size spider in a zoo or in the Amazon rain forest, where it is sometimes called a bird spider because it eats small birds, and frogs, too.

A tarantula's fangs are different from those of other spiders. Instead of working sideways like a pair of tongs or tweezers, they bite downward like a snake's fangs. Horror movies have made people think that the bite of a tarantula will kill a person. But venom that poisons small insects to death may only paralyze larger prey, and it may have no effect on people other than some swelling and pain that feels like a bee sting. According to official records, no adults in the United States have died from the bite of a tarantula. But if you are bitten, go to an emergency room right away because the venom is more dangerous to a child's smaller body than it is to a grown-up.

Never pick up a tarantula unless it's someone's pet, and even then, handle a tame tarantula carefully. Watch out for *urticating* (ER-ti-kay-ting) hairs on its abdomen. With one leg, a tarantula can flick off these stiff, prickly hairs, which will sting and burn your skin. A tarantula with bald spots on its belly is not an old spider. It's just been defending itself by dropping off its urticating hairs.

If you see a tarantula lying on its back with its legs in the air, it may be getting ready to molt. It's hard work to shed an exoskeleton. The spider has to tug each leg out of its old skin, like pulling fingers out of a tight glove. It can't stand up because the new legs are too soft at first. Smaller spiders usually hang from a single thread called a dragline while they molt.

Tarantulas don't need webs, but they do spin their silk into draglines, as well as soft linings for tunnels, doormats, sleeping bags, and cradles for their babies.

OTHER PRIMITIVE SPIDERS

FUNNEL WEB (AUSTRALIA)

MEXICAN RED KNEE

VELVET BLACK TARANTULA (SOUTH AMERICA)

CLOSELY RELATED POISONOUS SPIDERS

**RED-BACKED
SPIDER**

**FALSE WIDOW
SPIDER**

**MALMIGNATTE
SPIDER**

**KATIPO
SPIDER**

BLACK WIDOW

A widow is a woman whose husband has died. The name stuck to these shiny black spiders because the female sometimes eats the male after they mate — but not always. She eats the male only if she is starving, but many other spiders do this, too. The female's built-in instructions, or *instinct*, drive her to survive so that she can lay her eggs. When she is ready to mate, the female vibrates her cobweb in a way that tells the male to come close. If it's not the right signal, he stays away until the vibrations change. Once the male has made sure the eggs are fertilized, his work is done. He won't live much longer even if he escapes a hungry female's fangs.

Black widows don't go around looking for someone to bite. They hang upside down in their messy cobwebs, where they are seldom seen, and that is part of their danger. They choose a web site wherever there is a good supply of insects, which is usually where people are, too. Years ago, when most families had outhouses in the backyard instead of indoor bathrooms, black widow bites were more common because the spiders liked living where the fly supply never ran out.

The venom of a black widow is harmful to humans, but the male black widow is so small that his bite can't even break a person's skin. Even though the female's venom is powerful and plentiful, she seldom can inject enough venom to kill a grown-up. But her bite is dangerous, especially to children, and anyone who is bitten by a black widow should go quickly to a doctor or a hospital, where they have medicine called *antivenin*, which will stop the action of the poison.

Most black widows live in warm climates, but they have been found in all of America's forty-eight mainland states. Several black widows arrived in Buffalo, New York, in packages of grapes from California, and another traveled in a wheel cover of a car that was towed from Arizona.

Native Americans of the Gosuite tribe in Utah used to tip their arrows in a mixture of black widow venom and rattlesnake venom before they went out to hunt big game. They could have used the black widow venom alone because it is fifteen times more powerful than the rattler's venom.

EGG SAC

FEMALE ABOUT TO ENGAGE WITH MALE; POSSIBLE MATING PROCEDURE, WITH FEMALE THEN EATING MALE

BROWN RECLUSE

Part of the danger of the brown recluse spider is its plain brown body, which makes it look so harmless and which is so hard to see in a wood pile or sandbox. Some people call it a violin spider, because the marking on its back looks like a tiny violin. But if you get close enough to see the violin mark, make sure you don't touch this spider.

Recluse is the word used to describe a person who chooses to live alone, away from other people. This six-eyed spider weaves its sticky sheet web away from other spiders, but those places are under furniture, behind pictures, in empty boots, in jackets left hanging out-of-doors, or among boxes and tools in a shed. People put themselves in harm's way when they reach into these places without looking first, or without shaking out boots and jackets before putting them on. Caught against an arm and a sleeve, the spider bites in self-defense. Many people are bitten when they are sleeping or getting dressed.

The bite of a brown recluse doesn't usually kill, but it does a lot of damage. The bite itself may not be painful. Some people say they never even saw the spider, and didn't realize they'd been bitten until much later, when the wound turned black. Brown recluse venom causes living cells to die. The skin around the bite peels away as tissue is destroyed, leaving a large, deep wound that takes months to heal.

In spite of scary stories about them, the two most dangerous spiders in the United States, the black widow and the brown recluse, are less lethal (deadly) than lightning strikes or snakebites. Records kept in the United States from 1979 to 1991 show that 1,135 people were killed by lightning, 72 by snakebites, and 59 by bee stings. During those years, only 57 people were killed by spider bites, but before they died, 45 of those 57 people said that they had not seen a spider. Some of them may have been bitten by insects or scorpions.

OTHER POISONOUS SPIDERS

SYDNEY
FUNNEL WEB

BRAZILIAN
WANDERING SPIDER

SLENDER SAC SPIDER
(EUROPE, AFRICA, AND
NORTH AMERICA)

FACES AND JAWS—TWO OF THE DEADLIEST IN THE WORLD

**GIANT HUNTSMAN
(AUSTRALIA)**

**AUSTRALIAN
TRAP DOOR**

**BLACK CELLAR SPIDER (EUROPE, NORTH
AND SOUTH AMERICA, AND ASIA)**

PURSE WEB SPIDER

Duck hunters hide in shelters called blinds, where they can watch for ducks but where the birds can't see them. Purse web spiders hunt from blinds, too, but their shelters are blind for both hunter and prey. The spiders can't see out and the insects can't see in, yet the spiders are able to capture their food.

A purse web spider digs a tunnel in the ground with its tough jaws and lines it with silk. From the opening of the tunnel, the spider spins a dead-end tube of silk five or six inches long. In England, the purse spiders make tubes that lie flat on the ground, like the empty finger of a glove, hidden among leaves and twigs. The purse web spiders that live in the United States and Canada build a vertical tube that leans up against a tree trunk.

Once a tube is spun, the purse web spider crawls inside and waits. Imagine how the many footsteps of a centipede scurrying across the tube would cause the silk threads to vibrate. The spider doesn't have to see the centipede. It gets the message as clear as a dinner bell. With its big fangs, the spider stabs the centipede right through the silk purse, then sits back to wait while the venom works. When the centipede stops struggling, the spider chews a hole in the silk and drags its big meal into the tunnel. After the spider has finished eating, it tosses out the leftovers. Then it mends the rip by holding the edges of the torn tunnel together with its jaws while it spins a new patch of silk.

Spiders do not eat their food. They drink it. Most spiders are vomit-and-vacuum feeders. After they inject venom into their prey, they regurgitate (vomit) digestive juice into the holes made by the fangs, then wait for their meal to get gooey enough to drink. But like their bigger tarantula cousins, purse web spiders are crunch-and-slurp eaters. They have hard bumps called *endites* at the base of their pedipalps. Endites aren't real teeth, but they do the same job. A purse web spider crunches its prey to expose the soft inner tissue, then floods it with digestive juices that will turn it to liquid.

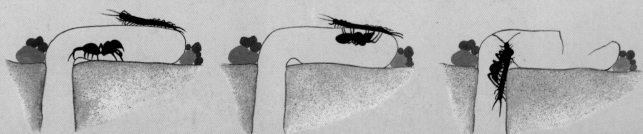

STAGE-BY-STAGE PROCESS OF PURSE WEB SPIDER CATCHING CENTIPEDE

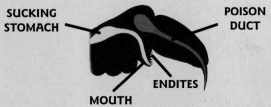

SUCKING
STOMACH

POISON
DUCT

ENDITES

MOUTH

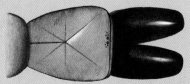

CARAPACE AND CHELICERAE
FROM ABOVE

**FEMALE SPITTING
SPIDER WITH EGGS**

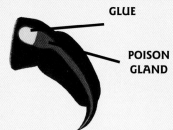

GLUE

POISON
GLAND

FACE

SPITTING SPIDER

Spit doesn't seem like much of a weapon for a hunter. But one small spider that may live in your basement can catch its dinner with spit faster than a fly can take off. A spitting spider's six pearly-white eyes aren't quite as sharp as those of other hunting spiders, and their legs don't carry them quite as fast. Even so, these tiny dome-shaped spiders manage to catch crickets and other prey that are much bigger and speedier than they are.

All spiders have glands that make venom, but the spitting spider's gland does double duty. The front part of the gland makes venom, and the back section makes glue. When the spider raises its head and squeezes the muscles on either side of this gland, two jets of sticky saliva squirt out through its fangs. By moving its jaws quickly from side to side, the spider sends the gummy glue in a zigzag pattern that falls across the prey like strapping tape. That pins down the insect long enough for the spider to stab it with venom. If it has caught a grasshopper that struggles a lot or a big wasp that might sting, the spider moves in cautiously and bites the insect's leg a few times. As soon as the insect stops moving, the spider takes off the bands of glue and drinks its juicy prey.

A spitting spider doesn't need a web, but it does spin a strong silk dragline, and the female makes a soft silk egg case. She is a very patient mother. She carries the egg case in her jaws until her hundreds of babies hatch several weeks later. During that time she doesn't eat.

Baby spiders molt at least once before they are ready to go ballooning. Then, with their bodies tipped tail end up, tiny streams of silk flow from their spinnerets. When a soft breeze tugs at the streamers, the spiderlings lift their feet and sail off like dandelion seeds. Some don't get farther than the next field, but others may be carried over mountains or oceans. Sailors have seen the baby ballooners a hundred miles from shore. When a volcano pokes up through the ocean to form a new island, spiders are often the first animals to arrive to set up housekeeping.

We use the word *gossamer* to mean delicate, loosely woven cloth, but it was invented long ago to describe wispy flights of spiderlings and filmy sheets of spider silk clinging to grass.

CAMOUFLAGE AND CRAB SPIDERS

FLOWER CRAB SPIDER

What looks like a flower but walks like a crab?

If you stare at a goldenrod, you might find the spider that answers the riddle. It may not be easy to see right away, because this little flower crab spider matches the color of the flower it is sitting on, or it may be standing on its head, imitating the center of the flower. It is called a crab spider because it looks like a miniature crab, scuttling sideways and backward, waving its front legs as though they were claws. Usually these spiders sit on flowers they already match, but like chameleons, they can change color. It's not a quick change, though. It may take two or three days for a pink crab spider to fade to white after it lands on a daisy.

All of the 200 different kinds of North American crab spiders work the day shift. Their eyes, like those of other day hunters, can follow anything that moves. But they also get information by touch. A crab spider can feel the slightest vibration of an insect landing on a leaf because each foot is covered with thirty hairs. And on each of those thirty hairs are five hundred to a thousand tinier hairs that pick up messages, too.

A French scientist, Jean-Henri Fabre, described the flower crab spider as "a cutthroat bandit, that steals up close to a bee, while she is filling her baskets with pollen, and her crop with nectar." With a sudden rush, this tiny spider bites the bee in the neck and hangs on. A few seconds later, when its strong venom has paralyzed the bee, the spider sucks the juice from the bee and tosses the carcass aside.

The female crab spider has no use for a web, but in May she spins a white silk, cone-shaped bag in and around twigs and dry leaves. She lays her eggs in this case, then closes it with a silk lid. Above the egg case, she weaves a silk canopy for herself as a kind of guardhouse, where she waits until the eggs are ready to hatch, in July. Then she cuts a window in the egg case, because it is too tough for baby spiders to break out of by themselves. It is the mother spider's last job before she dies. But the baby spiders molt and balloon away to find flowers of their own.

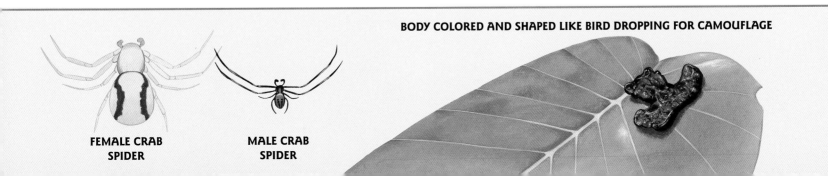

BODY COLORED AND SHAPED LIKE BIRD DROPPING FOR CAMOUFLAGE

FEMALE CRAB SPIDER

MALE CRAB SPIDER

BOLAS SPIDER

The tiny North American bolas spider can rope like a cowboy.

Bola means ball in Spanish, but it is also the word for a weapon made from a rope with a ball at the other end. South American cowboys are famous for their skill with this weapon. When the cowboy twirls the *bola* overhead and lets it fly through the air, the ball and rope tangle around a cow's legs and stop the animal in its tracks.

The spider makes its *bola* from a short thread of silk, tipped at one end with a gob of glue from its mouth. Holding this thread in one of its front legs, the spider swings it around, waiting for a fat moth to fly close enough to hit it. As if that isn't a hard enough way to get food, the spider hunts in the dark of night for one kind of small, brown moth. Scientists wondered how these spiders could ever find enough to eat under these conditions. After a lot of study, they found the spider's secret weapon. The bolas spider makes a scent that imitates the pheromone (FAIR-uh-moan) that the female moth sends out to attract male moths.

A pheromone is a chemical that is made by an animal as a way of sending messages. Some pheromones say, "Here I am! Come and mate with me." Others say, "Stay away" or "Danger! Come help me!"

As soon as the male moth gets a whiff of the bolas spider's fake "Here I am" pheromone, it is fooled into flying toward the spider that is sending the message. When the moth comes close enough, the spider swings the thread, and the moth gets stuck on the gob of glue. The spider quickly hauls in the surprised moth, then wraps it in silk threads that will hold it for a later dinner.

Even with its odd way of hunting, a bolas spider manages to catch two or three juicy moths in an evening, which is about what an orb web spider can trap in its nightly web. That's plenty to keep its appetite satisfied.

NET-THROWING SPIDER DROPS STICKY WEB ON PREY PASSING UNDERNEATH

BOLAS SPIDER HUNTING

JUMPING SPIDERS

A small, glowing green Australian jumping spider hunts big game. After a mighty four-inch leap, it sinks its fangs into a dragonfly's neck. Even if this huge insect takes off, the spider hangs on until its venom works and the dragonfly makes a crash landing.

Four inches may not seem like much of a jump, but it's a huge distance for an animal half an inch long. That would be like a five-foot-tall person leaping over six cars lined up end to end. All the 4,000 different jumping spiders stalk their prey like cats. When they leap, they push off with strong hind legs, like a swimmer taking off from a starting block. They are wanderers, so they make no webs, traps, or snares. But they do use silk to make cradles for eggs and nets to sleep in — and they always fasten a dragline before they leap, in case they miss their target.

Jumpers live in almost every part of the world. One species holds the record for high-altitude living. It was found on an ice field 22,000 feet up Mt. Everest. The spiders had been delivered by wind, swept up the mountain from habitats in the valley below. In tropical rain forests, some jumping spiders are hard to find because they blend with dead leaves. Others have spots of dazzling red and blue, and one looks like an ant. A black-and-white zebra jumping spider, no bigger than a raisin, may live on your windowsill, where it catches mosquitoes and gnats. If you let one of these stocky little zebra spiders jump on your finger, it won't hurt you. With its two biggest eyes, it will follow every move you make, and you may understand why one scientist calls jumping spiders the teddy bears of the spider world.

You might think that all spiders would have terrific vision with so many eyes, but most spiders are practically blind. They catch their food at night, more by touch than sight. But if jumping spiders are kept in the dark, they won't grab a fly even if they bump into one. They hunt in daylight because their eyes are different from those of the night hunters. A jumping spider's two big eyes are like telephoto lenses that zero in on moving insects, and its six smaller eyes are wide-angle lenses, which judge distance. Most animals see an image on television as a jumble of moving dots. But Dr. Mark Moffat, who studies animal behavior, says that jumping spiders see television in color as we do, and they pay special attention when they watch spiders and insects on the screen.

APACHE SPIDER

ZEBRA SPIDER

PANTROPICAL SPIDER

PAINTER'S JUMPING
SPIDER
(AUSTRALIA)

SPEAR-JAWED
SPIDER

FACE OF TYPICAL
JUMPING SPIDER

CELLAR SPIDERS

Long-legged cellar spiders live in almost every house, but not always in the cellar. They crawl up walls and across ceilings in search of shelter from too much heat or cold. In some parts of the country, people call them daddy longlegs, and it's easy to see why when you compare them with the real daddy longlegs pictured on the next page. To avoid the mix-up, it's easier to use this spider's scientific name, *Phlocus* (pronounced FLOW-kus).

Hanging upside down by its long, skinny legs, *Phlocus* looks frail and fragile, and its messy web looks as though it had been tossed together in a hurry. But *Phlocus* is a sturdy survivor. It's also a pirate.

When an insect is snared in its web, *Phlocus* goes into action. With its second and third pairs of legs, it rolls the insect back and forth, while its fourth legs pull silk out of the spinnerets and throw it around the insect. If the prey is too big or struggling too much, *Phlocus* adds a few extra lines to anchor it to the web. After it bites the wrapped insect, the spider settles down to eat.

Phlocus turns pirate when it goes out for dinner. It can be dangerous for one spider to invade another spider's web, because both of them have fangs and venom. *Phlocus* sets up an ambush. It sneaks onto another spider's web, then shakes and shivers and generally acts crazy. This movement makes the web vibrate. When the unsuspecting owner of the web rushes to see what's been trapped, *Phlocus* attacks, eating its victim along with anything else it finds in the web — the spider's eggs or wrapped prey the owner has been saving for later. Sometimes *Phlocus* gets lucky and happens upon a web whose owner isn't home. Then it gets its take-out meal without a battle.

Not all spiders can move around in a foreign web without getting stuck. *Phlocus* can because its legs are so long that it can step over sticky threads. And if it does get stuck, it can pull itself out easily because it walks on the very tips of its skinny feet.

The strangest thing about *Phlocus* is the way it defends itself. Instead of running away when it's threatened, it spins. It clutches its web with its claws and spins its body around and around so fast that it's just a blur. That's usually enough to make any attacker give up and go away.

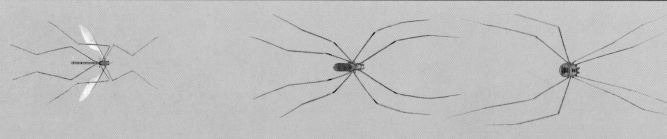

CRANE FLY   PHLOCUS   HARVESTMAN

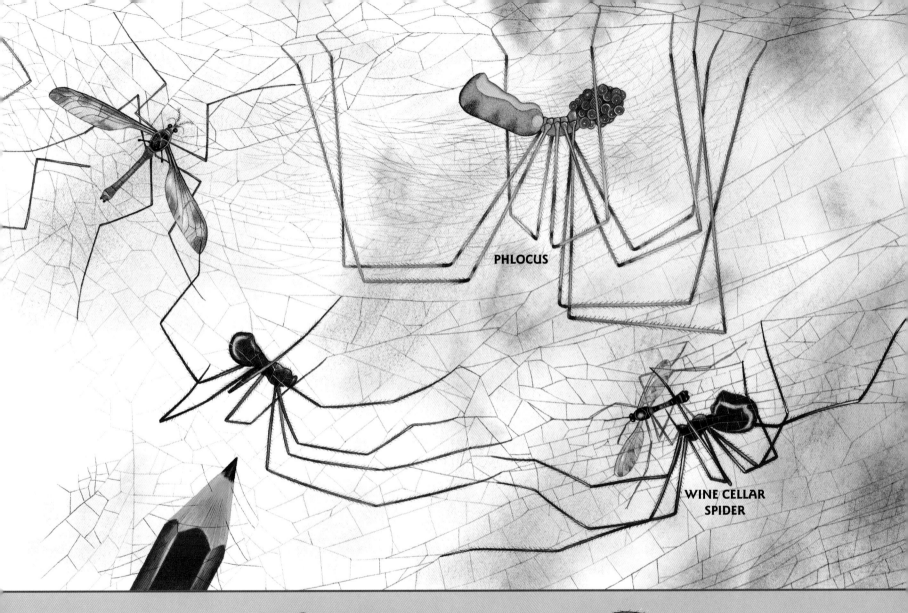

PHLOCUS

WINE CELLAR
SPIDER

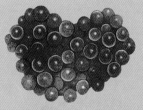

EGG SAC

FACE

29

DADDY LONGLEGS

Prancing along on its eight spindly legs, a daddy longlegs may look like a spider, but it's neither a spider nor an insect. It is an arthropod, related to both. It's included in this book because it is so often mistaken for one or the other.

In 1665, when Robert Hooke invented his first microscope, one of the things he looked at was a daddy longlegs, which he called an air crab or shepherd spider. In those days, farmers believed that if they lost a cow, all they had to do was look for a shepherd spider. If they followed the direction in which its second pair of legs was pointing, they'd find the cow. Because so many of these little creatures were seen at harvesttime, they were also called harvest spiders or harvestmen and sometimes father longlegs, which eventually became daddy longlegs.

If you grab a daddy longlegs, one of its legs can easily break off. The best way to catch one is to hold out your hand and let it walk up your arm. It will tickle, but it won't sting and it won't bite. It has no fangs and no venom, although it does have a pair of glands that give off an awful smell. And it makes no silk — not for a web, not even for a dragline.

The two round, shiny black eyes perched on top of daddy longlegs' one-piece body don't see much more than dark and light, and they only look sideways. Daddy longlegs finds food and senses danger with its second pair of legs, which are longer than the others and used as feelers. If it loses a leg or one feeler, it can still get around and find food. But if both feelers are gone, the daddy longlegs will starve.

Even with no venom and no silk, a daddy longlegs can trap a juicy moth and keep it caged between its legs. Then with all eight legs doing push-ups, it pumps its body up and down to smack the moth to death. But that's not the only way it gets a meal. Daddy longlegs are *scavengers*. They eat leftover carcasses in spiderwebs, and they also eat plants. One scientist who studies daddy longlegs feeds them bacon, cornmeal, fruit, and bits of marshmallow as a special treat. Daddy longlegs need a lot of water, and you can often find them drinking from puddles after a rain.

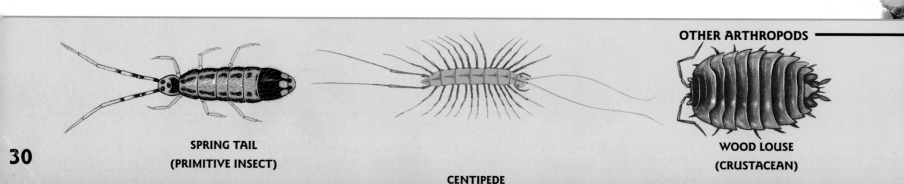

OTHER ARTHROPODS

SPRING TAIL
(PRIMITIVE INSECT)

CENTIPEDE

WOOD LOUSE
(CRUSTACEAN)

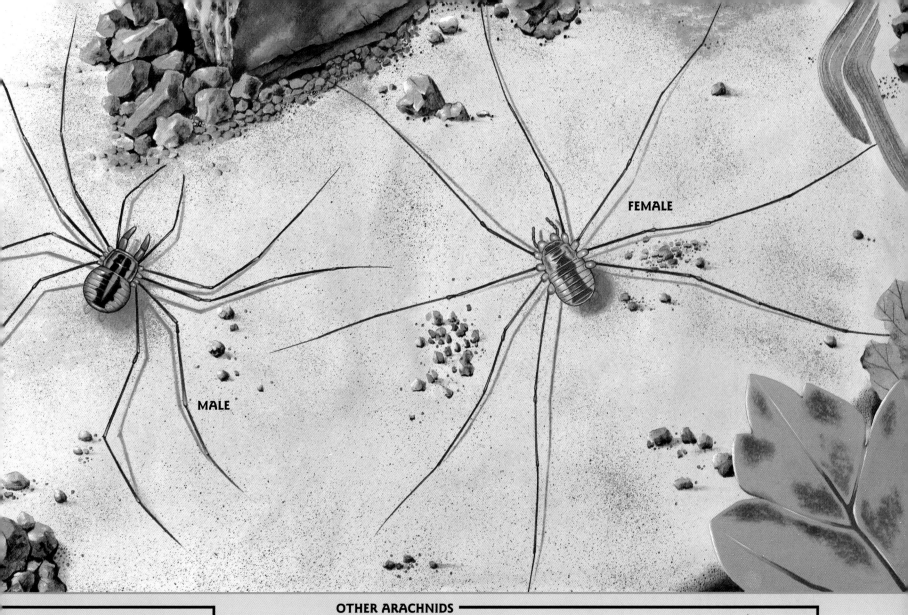

FEMALE

MALE

OTHER ARACHNIDS

SHEEP TICK

WATER
MITE

VELVET MITE

PSEUDOSCORPION

GLOSSARY

Antivenin: the serum made from an animal's venom that counteracts the effects of the poison

Arthropoda: the group of animals with exoskeletons, including spiders, insects, and crabs

Bola: the Spanish word for ball

Book lungs: a chamber of page-like tissue on a spider's abdomen that it uses for breathing

Cephalothorax: the combination of head and thorax that makes up the front part of a spider's body

Chelicerae: the jaws of a spider

Endite: hard, tooth-like projections on a spider's chelicerae

Exoskeleton: the hard outer shell of a spider, insect, or other arthropod

Instinct: behavior based on automatic reactions rather than learned

Pedipalps: small leg-like projections on a spider's head; used as feelers and for grasping

Pheromone: a chemical signal produced by an animal to attract a mate or prey

Scavenger: an animal that feeds on dead animals and other leftovers

Species: a group of plants or animals made up of related individuals that can produce young of the same kind

Spinnerets: the organs on a spider's abdomen that spin silk

Swathing: wrapping or enfolding with some material, such as spider silk

Tension: the act of stretching or straining something

Urticating hairs: stiff, stinging hairs, as on a tarantula

FURTHER READING

For Young Readers

Spiders Near and Far, by Jennifer Owings Dewey (Dutton, 1993).

Spiders and Their Kin, by Herbert W. Levi and Lorna R. Levi (Golden Press, 1990).

For Older Readers

The Book of the Spider, From Arachnophobia to the Love of Spiders, by Paul Hillyard (Random House, 1994).

Spiders of the World, by Rod and Ken Preston (Facts on File, 1994).